Kung Fu Kid

Written by
Rob Waring and **Maurice Jamall**

Before You Read

to bow

arm

to fight

face

to hit

leg

to jump

hurt

to kick

small

to laugh

tall

to move

In the story

Adib

Ray

Mike

Scott

Kung Fu
teacher

"Are you new?" a boy asks Adib.

Adib is at the kung fu class. It is his first day in the class. There are many people there. They are waiting for the teacher.

"Yes, I am," Adib says. "I'm Adib."

"Hi, I'm Ray," the boy says.

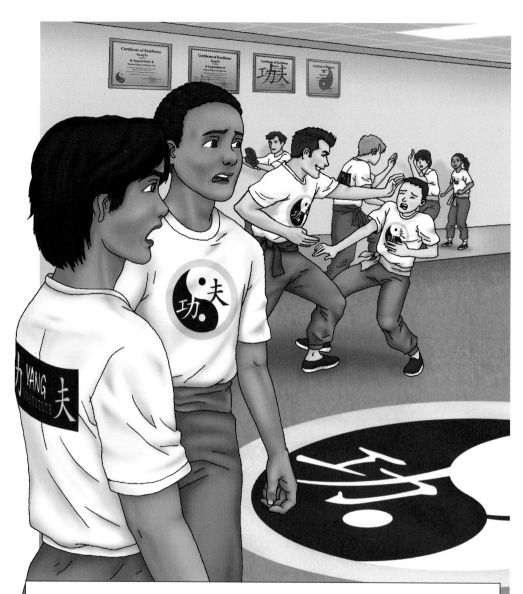

Adib looks at the other students. Some big boys are fighting some small boys.

Ray talks to Adib about one of the boys. "That's Mike Henson," says Ray. "He's very good at kung fu."

"Yes, but the boy is too small," says Adib. "He will get hurt."

"Yes, I know," says Ray. "Mike likes to hurt smaller boys."

Adib is getting ready for class. He is watching another boy.
"Who's that?" Adib asks Ray.
"Scott Nash," says Ray. "He's very good, but he likes to hit people, too."
"I can see," says Adib. The small boy is hurt.

"Stop that!" Adib says to Scott. "Stop!"
Scott stops fighting with the boy. "Why? Who are you?" asks Scott.
"I'm Adib Murad," he says. "That boy can't fight you. You are bigger than he is. You'll hurt him."
"Then you come here and fight me," says Scott. "Come on!"
"Not now," says Adib. "The teacher's here."

The kung fu teacher bows to the students. The students bow to the teacher.

Scott pushes Adib. The teacher sees Scott push Adib.

Adib falls down in front of the teacher. Everyone is very surprised.

Mike and Scott laugh. But the teacher is not laughing.

The teacher says to Adib, "You're a new student. What's your name?" he asks.

"Adib Murad," he replies.

The teacher says, "Do you know kung fu, Adib?"

"A little," says Adib. "But I want to learn more."

"Okay, Adib," says the teacher. "But first I want to see your kung fu."

The teacher looks at the class.

"Who wants to fight Adib?" he asks.

"I will fight him," says a boy. It is Scott's friend, Mike. Mike is bigger and stronger than Adib.

Mike looks down at Adib. Mike wants to hurt him.

"Okay Mike, you can fight him," says the teacher.

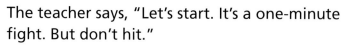

The teacher says, "Let's start. It's a one-minute fight. But don't hit."
The fight starts. Mike tries to kick Adib, but Adib is too fast. He stops the kick, and Mike falls down. Adib is small, but he is very good at kung fu. Everybody is very surprised.

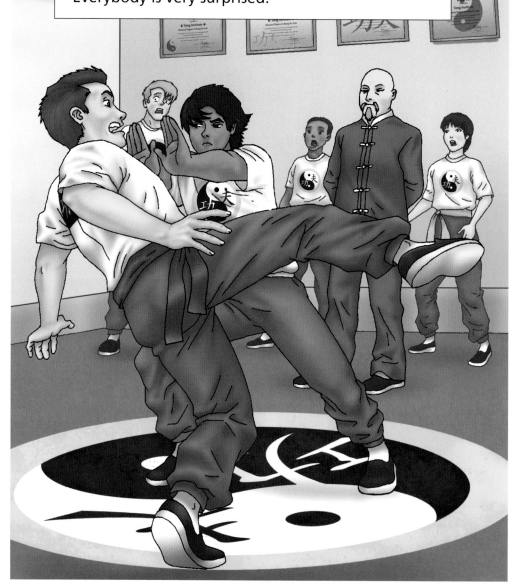

"I'm sorry," says Adib. "Are you okay?" he asks Mike.

But Mike gets up. He is very angry, and he wants to hurt Adib.

"Stop!" says the teacher. "Don't fight!"

But Mike does not listen. He tries to hit Adib in the face, but Adib is too fast.

Adib stops Mike's arm. He pushes Mike in the back, and he falls again.

Scott watches Adib.

"You are very good, Adib," says the teacher. "You don't hurt people. Very good."

"Umm. . . , thank you, but I want you to teach me more," says Adib.

The teacher says, "Let's see you fight with our number one student. Scott, please come here."

Scott comes to Adib. He looks worried!

Scott says, "I'm sorry, my leg hurts today."

"Really, Scott?" says the teacher. He doesn't think Scott is hurt. The teacher says, "Scott, do you want to go home, or fight Adib?"

"Umm. . . , I want to fight," he says. Scott knows Adib is good at kung fu.

"So, please fight Adib. But do not hit," says the teacher. Some of the students start laughing at Scott because he is worried.

Scott looks at Adib. Adib looks at Scott. Scott is taller than Adib, and he is stronger, too.

"Are you ready, little boy?" asks Scott.

"Yes," Adib says. "I'm ready. And I'm not a little boy!"

"Wait. Don't start," says the teacher.

But Scott does not listen. He runs and jumps at Adib. He tries to kick Adib. Adib is faster than Scott. He moves away, and Scott falls down.

Scott knows Adib is very good. He cannot hit Adib. Adib is too good. Scott is sitting on the floor. He doesn't want to fight Adib now.

He says, "*Ouch*! My leg. I can't fight now. I'm hurt."

Everybody is surprised. They know he is not hurt.

Scott goes out of the room. Everybody knows he is not hurt. They laugh at him because he does not want to fight Adib. "Very good, Adib," says the teacher. "You are smaller than Scott, but you are faster. You are good at kung fu."
"Thank you," Adib replies.
The teacher says, "You are a good student, and a good teacher, too."